KU-615-111

Contents

Introduction

'More marriages ending in divorce.'

'Children suffer when parents separate, say researchers.'

'Trouble ahead for sons of "broken homes".'

We've all seen the headlines. Has there ever been an aspect of life surrounded by more emotive and conflicting reports than divorce and separation? I doubt it.

If you are a parent facing the prospect of separating from your partner but want to do the best for your children, then your head must be swimming.

When you are struggling with the reality and finality of a divorce or separation, it's easy to start to believe that this will cause immeasurable damage to your children. After all, isn't divorce and separation the bogeyman we have all grown up with? Isn't it the deciding factor in everything in a child's life, from how they form their own relationships and how they do at school to whether or not they can hold down a job?

Well, no actually, it isn't. The one overriding nugget of wisdom I have learnt through researching this book, talking to dozens of parents and relationship experts, is that even though a child's parents are separated, it doesn't have to be the most critical factor in a child's future happiness, health and wealth – even if some recent newspaper reports would have us believe otherwise.

What matters most is how this undoubtedly traumatic turn of events is handled, how the parents conduct themselves in front of their children, how they relate to each other, what they say about them and how they work together to make things work.

The fact that things can work doesn't make good copy for today's newspaper columnists, but if the experience of many of the parents I have spoken to is anything to go by, this is the truth of the matter.

For some children, where there have been a lot of arguments or even violence, then the end of the relationship may be a relief. There are even parents who will readily admit that they feel they see more of their children after a separation than they did before. They no longer feel they have to avoid their home life but can nurture or welcome their children in a new family set-up – free from the complications that were making their life a misery before the split happened.

A new found confidence, sense of purpose or direction in life – not to mention a new relationship – can have a major positive effect on parenting skills. It is actually okay to acknowledge this, to understand that a happy parent can mean happy kids. There's nothing selfish in wanting the best for yourself and your children – and this can mean being away from your former partner.

The days of staying together for the children are well and truly over – for every story of drunken yobs from 'broken homes' on the rampage, highlighted by our so very sensitive media, there are many more families away from the spotlight doing just fine.

Like the rest of us – married, divorced, separated, young, old, rich, poor, single parent or co-habiting – they are just doing the best they can in the circumstances.

You may not know yet how resilient or adaptable your children are, but isn't this what we are told so very often? Children can and do accept change – so long as they know they are still loved and secure. The root of your relationship with your children – built on unconditional love – is not changing.

Every family, whatever their circumstances, and even if they stay together, will go through its ups and downs. Redundancy, bereavement, crime – these terrible things happen to all of us. Divorce and separation does not have to be the end of the world. Understanding this can be key to your future happiness and that of your family.

This book is here to help. Whether you are a parent, step-parent or grandparent, the information included here can help you chart a course through what could be the stormiest waters of your family life.

Forget the guilt trip. All any parent wants for their children is the best – and that includes those parents who decide to go their separate ways. As well as the types of reports illustrated so far, further research led by Dr Bren Neale of Leeds University actually says that children of divorced parents do okay. Well, some do badly, some do fine and some do great – just like the children of parents who stay together.

> 'It can't be better for an unhappy couple to stay together... I should know, my mum and dad stayed together too long. These days I'm a single mum and that's the way I like it.'
>
> Caroline, mum to Rhiannon, 12.

In other words, divorce does not have to be the ultimate bogeyman for your children's development. Tell that nagging voice, which insists that separating from your partner also means long-term 'damage' for your children, to take a running jump.

It doesn't have to be that way.

Findings over years of academic surveys, relationship polls and important research have been very mixed. There was a time when the accepted wisdom was that children were undoubtedly better off after their parents parted. Who would prefer living with two unhappy, squabbling parents to one secure, content and optimistic one? But then we were told of the potential negative effects. Back to square one.

These days relationship experts will tell you that it is not the fact that their parents are divorced that makes children unhappy in the long-term. The immediate pain and distress of a separation is hard for all involved – and that includes the adults. So we can only begin to imagine what children feel. No matter how hard we try, and how much we plan ahead, difficult feelings will follow. There is no magic wand to wave away their sense of loss.

But this despair as their old world changes into a new one is not an insurmountable summit to conquer. Although short-term distress at the time of separation is common, this usually lessens and any long-term emotional damage typically only affects a minority of youngsters.

According to latest statistics for England and Wales, the number of couples divorcing in 2006 was 132,562, with more than half involving at least one child, 20% of whom were under five. Nobody wants their children to become such a statistic.

Actually those latest figures, from the Office of National Statistics, are lower than for the previous year. You may consider this a positive development, but this apparent downturn in break-ups should be viewed with suspicion. Fewer people are getting married now in the first place. Of course, the issues facing cohabiting couples who part are just as pressing as for those with a marriage certificate languishing somewhere in a sideboard drawer.

Whatever has gone awry in the partnership, both parents still have a crucial role to play in their children's lives.

'These days, lots of children brought up in single parent homes have a hugely supportive extended family. With all that love, it's no wonder that they grow up as well balanced and stable as any other children.'

Claire, mum to Becky, nine.

The feelings a child will have to come to terms with may include:

- An overriding sense of loss – being parted from one of their parents can mean losing much more than the proximity of that relationship.
- Feeling a conflict of loyalty. When they are with one parent, they feel guilty about not being with the other, and vice versa.
- Fears over being singled out as different by other children.
- Uncertainty about the future – surely if one parent can leave, can't the other?
- Anger – with one or both parents, or themselves.
- Blame – it must be their fault, right?
- Rejection – why has mum or dad done this to them and why do they feel torn?

Most children long to get back to normal and for their parents to be together again. Even if the marriage or partnership has been very tense or violent, children may still have mixed feelings about the separation.

So it's back to the research. According to work academics from Leeds University, it is not the changes brought about by divorce or separation that make the difference, but the ways in which those changes are handled.

They found that:

- The absence of a parent is not the most important aspect of a separation for children's progress in the world.
- The age at which children experience that separation is not crucial.
- In direct contrast to received wisdom, boys are not more adversely affected than girls.

This book aims to help parents who are in the midst of coming to terms with the heartbreaking decision to part, in a bid to help their children cope and move towards becoming part of an albeit new and different, but safe and loving family set-up. Children know and understand a lot more than we give them credit for.

I hope that the advice and insights included in this book can help minimise the emotional fallout of the end of a relationship between two people who, at one time, thought enough of each other to have a child together. If you are a carer or teacher, this information can also help you understand what a child is going through.

Chapter One

Breaking the News

'I'm about to divorce my wife of eight years. We have worked really hard to stop this happening – for the sake of our son – but actually, we worry now that staying together for as long as we have may have caused more upset than a clean break. I hate to think of him hearing us arguing or feeling an almost tangible tension when we have all been at home. Also, I've stayed at work when I could have come home. There is no way that my son will suffer from his mum and dad breaking up as we will be happier apart. I'll miss him terribly as he will live with his mum, but far prefer that to the alternative.'
Alan, dad to Rhys, five.

So you are going your separate ways. How to let your children know can be as worrying as the impending impact of this life-changing news.

You already know there is no easy way. Now you have to work out a way of breaking the news that will minimise the emotional fallout for your children.

Of course they aren't stupid – how much they already know of the problems mum and dad have been experiencing will depend on what you have already said and how you have acted in front of them. Even if they suspect something is afoot, they'll be hoping they are wrong.

One of the most important steps to take when breaking the news to your children is to accept yourself that it's over. It may sound obvious, but it's not. You have to be sure that it's the right time to tell your children. If you are still secretly clinging on to a belief that things can be fixed, that your partner will change their mind, or that the two of you can still work things out, then now is not the right time.

Whether you are the one who has been the driving force behind a decision to split or not, there could be reasons why there may still be a misapprehension about what the future holds.

'It's not the divorce that causes any lasting emotional damage, it's the parents involved. I'm glad that my parents faced up to the fact that they couldn't continue to live under the same roof.'

Jonathan, now 28.

'I can still remember the moment my mum told us dad had been having an affair. I was only 11 but it was devastating. She took me and my sister to school and came into the classroom to tell my teacher. I remember standing there with tears streaming down my cheeks.

'I remember being in the kitchen and watching Coronation Street on the TV. Someone was getting divorced and the kids were being asked where they wanted to live. The same thing was happening to me. I was desperately unhappy. But somewhere along the line it was all swept under the carpet. If I'm honest, I wish we'd been shielded from that. If mum and dad had really split up there would have been more support from them, more discussions, but one minute they were splitting up and the next they weren't. Nothing further was said. It was all very awkward. I wish they'd explained what happened afterwards.'

Shirley, mum to Hannah and Lauren, nine.

As you can see, this indecision – or denial – can be terribly misleading, upsetting and confusing for the children in your relationship. If you do get back together after telling your children of the life-changing decision to part, the pain and hurt that announcement causes cannot be taken away.

A child taken in tears to their head teacher's room while their mum or dad explains that they are no longer going to be together will still remember that pain 30 years later. They will still remember that they felt torn, that they had the impossible task of choosing which parent to live with.

Parents who look back at the moment of sharing the news of a break-up with their young family talk of the pain it caused and say that it can still make them cry as they remember the crumpled faces of their children, or the looks of confusion and pain. Would you really want to put your children through that if it wasn't for real?

So to be sure of not sending mixed messages to your children, make sure you aren't kidding yourself with those same mixed messages. Now is no time to fool yourself.

However, don't leave your children not knowing what is happening. While it is inevitably painful to learn that their parents are separating, there is much that can be done to lessen this hurt as time goes on. The uncertainty and confusion that follows when children are given the wrong signals, leading to a 'Will they? Won't they?' type scenario, can drag on and chip away at their happiness for a long time to come.

Honesty is the best policy

Suspecting that their parents are having problems doesn't prepare children for the potentially devastating announcement that they are going to separate.

The most important factor in how you tell your children, alongside dignity, calmness and compassion, is honesty.

When your children ask a question, you must answer truthfully, as much as you are able, without bitterness, resentment or anger creeping in.

When should you tell them?

There may never be a right time, but you should plan ahead as to what to say, when, where and how.

Make your children feel valued and loved.

Make them feel that they are the central part of all future plans.

Don't speak too soon

Do you know what you are going to do after you and your partner go your separate ways? If not, now may not be the time to tell your children.

Children need security, so being able to tell them as much as you can about what is going to happen now and in the future will help them adjust and will help their initial reaction.

Think about what they have going on in their lives and if these events may affect how they take the news. Are they coming up for any changes in their life anyway, such as a new school, exams or shows?

'Children affected by the tribulations of divorce are better off than those who continue to live in unhappy families where the parents stay together. Why can't these parents find the courage to do what they know is best?'

Jane, mum to Elizabeth, 12.

Don't leave it too late

How does telling your children fit in with telling everyone else? Just like in the words of the song, you don't want them to be the last to know, yet asking them to keep it a secret is an extra burden that they can do without.

Find a balance. Don't tell too many people first but don't put your children in the difficult position of not being able to say anything to their friends.

What should you say?

This needs to be planned with your partner, if at all possible. Ask yourself what questions you think will be asked and how you can answer them. By doing this you are minimising the potential of 'mixed messages' arising, which would lead to further upset.

Put yourself in your children's shoes. How would you want to be told? A stark announcement sat around the breakfast table just before everyone dashes off to playgroup, nursery, school or work isn't going to cut it.

How old the children are will also shape their individual experience and will determine how much they understand. Younger children can be especially hard hit as they struggle to comprehend not only the fact that mum and dad don't want to be together, but also what this means for their daily lives.

How much should you tell them?

This can be one of the most difficult decisions. With younger children it can be easy to assume that they understand more than they do or can cope with the news. You know your children better than anyone; take their age, intelligence and maturity into account and formulate your words according to these important factors.

With older children it may be more uncomfortable as there may be more questions, more accusations or more emotions on display. You have to make what you say objective. Under no circumstances should you seek to apportion blame to one or other parent. Your children love you both and as such cannot be expected to take sides.

With younger children you will need to help them understand that because one parent is leaving the family home, it doesn't follow that this means their other parent will also leave. Whatever the age of the children you have to assure them that moving out doesn't mean moving out of their lives. If you or your partner are moving to a new address or into a new relationship then the next step will be helping your children understand what all of this will mean.

But for now, as you broach the subject of their parents splitting up, the most important reassurance is that you both still love them very much and always will. Yes it's a simplistic message but in this case that's what children need.

Do say:

Mum doesn't love dad as much as she used to because we are arguing a lot about things. We have tried our best to do what we can so we won't argue but it hasn't helped. We have discussed this a lot and have decided that we would both be happier if we lived in different places.

We still care for each other but want different things to make us happy. None of this is your fault and we both still love you very much.

Don't say:

It's best that mum and dad live apart now as it is better for all of us. We can't stop rowing and everyone will be much happier if I move out. You want us to be happy, don't you and you want to be happy? If we live apart, you will be happier.

Don't say:

Mum is really upsetting dad at the moment and it's making her sad. Mum can't forgive dad for something that has happened, but we can't tell you what it is.

Do say:

Mum doesn't love dad any more because we have both changed. Dad has told Mum that he has met someone else. There are going to be some changes and dad is going to move out.

Do you think there is much difference between the two examples in the first set? At first glance it may appear not, but the language is much more subtle in the first example. It is gentler and there is no blame attached.

In the second example, there is far too much emphasis on future happiness and how this decision is the deciding factor. This may be true as explained in the introduction, but that's not likely to be a comforting or easy to understand thought for a child being told their parents are splitting up.

They must not be told how they 'should' feel – they are very unlikely to accept that they will feel happier and when they don't, they will feel even worse. You can't expect a younger child to accept this as they are most likely to be confused and upset. An older child may resent the way this statement is put together, as if you are shifting the blame of an adult decision on to the whole family's shoulders. This decision comes from the two of you first and foremost, so find the right words to get that message across.

Again, there may not appear to be much difference in the second set of examples, but there is a huge gulf between them. Don't tell your children that you are keeping something from them, this will only cause greater anxiety. This example also breaks the vital rule of not apportioning blame. Telling your children that one parent's actions are blatantly upsetting the other, is a recipe for further upset.

In the final example, the decision to part is portrayed as a joint one, despite the news that the father is set to move out. Telling your children that one of their parents has met someone else is not too much information. Although it is bound to lead to a lot of questions, honesty remains the best policy.

Openness is key as is using the right language for the age of the child.

If you have children of different ages then you have to be prepared to explain what is happening more than once, and to answer everyone's questions.

Do it together

Put your own problems to one side – whatever the difficulties. Sue Atkins, relationship expert and founder of Positive Parents, says 'You may not have been a united front while married, but you and your partner must take this opportunity – for the good of your children – to work together.'

Sue lists what she considers 'critical' questions or 'key messages' for those approaching their children about this sensitive stage.

She says you should consider:

- Your children's need to feel reassured that you'll both always be their parents and will always love them.

- Their need to express themselves – this may include anger, silence, denial, bravado, or pleading.

- You need to weigh up whether each parent tells each child separately or all together. If you can manage to speak to them together, this gives an opportunity for them to see that you're not blaming each other, that they don't have to take sides and that you're both still there for them.

- Think about the sort of questions your children are likely to ask. 'Will we still see you and spend time with you?', 'Who will take us to football training?', 'Who will we live with and where will we live?', 'Will we have to change school?', 'Will we still see Grandma?'. You need to explain that at the moment you don't have all the answers but reassure them that you'll have more clarity and answers soon and they don't need to worry.

For more information visit www.positive-parents.com.

Don't play the 'blame game'

The parting doesn't have to be anyone's fault. Whatever you feel, you should try to overcome the mentality that tells you one partner or other is to blame. This will help you find ways to avoid your children thinking they have to take sides.

Whatever has gone on between you and your partner, you need to set your differences aside and join forces to show your children a united front. Take time to plan what you are going to say and, hopefully, talk to the children together.

If your partner won't co-operate

You have to give it your best shot – and that means staying calm. However sad or angry you are feeling with your partner, try not to let any strain or bitterness creep into your voice, words, or actions as you break the news.

'You need to weigh up whether each parent tells each child separately, or all together. If you can manage to speak to them together, this gives an opportunity for them to see that you're not blaming each other, that they don't have to take sides, and that you're both still there for them.'

Sue Atkins, relationship expert.

Pre-school children

- Give them a hug and tell them as simply as you can what is happening.
- Tell them you love them and it is not their fault.
- Explain that this happens to lots of parents.
- Be clear about what the living arrangements will be.

If the question of whose fault it is comes up, assure them that it is absolutely not their fault. Tell them there is no way they should blame themselves and that doing so would be a waste of time!

- Be prepared for them to get upset, but stay as calm as you can.
- Explain that just because mummy and daddy no longer want to be together, this doesn't mean that they don't love their children any more.
- Emphasise that both parents' feelings for their children will not change.
- Tell them that their friends will understand and that they are no different to other children just because their parents are separating.

Children aged five to 10

- As above, the most important thing is to reassure them that you both still love them very much.
- Encourage them to ask as many questions as they like and answer them as truthfully as you can.
- If they start to cry, tell them that this is okay.
- Be sure to explain that this is a definite situation – children of this age may think they can plot a reconciliation.

Children aged 10 to 12

- They may be angry. They may reject you. They may fly off the handle.
- Be prepared for this reaction and reassure them that they are very loved and will continue to be loved by both parents, despite new living arrangements.

- Stay calm and, as above, answer their questions as truthfully as you can without apportioning blame.

Teenagers

- Just because your children are older, don't be fooled into thinking the news of a break-up will be any less monumental.
- Again, encourage them to share their feelings and to feel as involved as possible.
- Be as calm, patient and caring as you can, even if they lash out.
- If they 'clam up' do all you can to help them explain how they feel, either now or as time goes on.

See chapter 7 for more information.

Outside support

Let school and any clubs or activity groups know what is happening at home. They can be more mindful of how your children are behaving and let you know if they are outwardly upset or become withdrawn.

Encourage your children to stick to their normal routines and activities as much as possible. Tell them how important it is for them to continue to see their friends and talk to them about how they feel.

See chapter 8 for more information on outside support.

Action points

Encourage your children to have a say in what they want to see happen, once they've accepted that their parents will no longer live together.

Make sure that other important people in your children's lives – their relatives, teachers and friends – also know what is going on so that they can understand and support them if needs be.

'My parents are divorced. They separated when I was nine. I learnt lessons in life that I would not have learnt otherwise. I know that nobody is responsible for my actions but me. Even though my parents decided to no longer live together, they both made it clear they still loved me.'

Helen, now 32.

Summing Up

- It's best to tell your children together.
- Plan what to say as much as you can.
- Honesty is a must.
- Don't let any resentment towards your partner show.
- Don't speak too soon!

Chapter Two

Dealing With
Their Reaction

How do children react?

Confusion, guilt, sadness, depression, grief, silence and anger – these are all possible reactions. Some children may exhibit some of them, and others the full range. Some children may seem perfectly 'okay' with what is happening, as if they are taking it in their stride.

This may be an attempt to please you or to do what they think is right, not wanting to cause further upset. They may even go out of their way to be 'as good as gold' in an effort to make things better.

Tell them that it's okay to be upset, to be angry and sad. Tell them you are there for them and you can listen to everything they have to say. Ask them to be as honest as they can with you, to discuss their feelings and let you know exactly what they are worried about.

Expect them also to become more clingy as they seek greater security. Who could blame them? Importantly, though, how these feelings are expressed will differ from child to child. They may bombard you with questions about what's going to happen now. They may become withdrawn, believing that nobody understands what they are going through. A bright, bubbly child may become uncharacteristically quiet because they don't know what to say.

The younger the child, the greater the confusion may be. They might not even understand the meaning of divorce or separation. You have to help them understand while showing them it's not the end of their world.

Children may think that if one parent leaves the family home, then the other may follow. Tell them firmly that this is not the case.

Give them time. Surround them with love. Explain all you can and reassure them at every turn that the parent they are living with isn't going anywhere and the parent who has moved away still loves them very much.

Maintain routines

Children need structure in their lives. As one part of the family structure is eroded, the routines and stability that make up the rest of their daily lives take on a greater importance.

Pull out all the stops to make sure that you can maintain this normality as much

While your children are reeling from the news that their parents are separating, let them feel safe in the routines of going to bed at the same time, being reminded to clear their plates away and watching a DVD on a Friday night – or whatever particular family habits you have adopted.

'Children need structure in their lives. As family structure is eroded, the routines and stability that make up the rest of their daily lives take on a greater importance.'

Encourage them to ask questions

Every child will have their own way of reacting and questions they want answering, not least 'Why?' – 'Why our family?', 'Why me?' , 'Why now?', 'Why is this happening?'.

Telling your children that you and their other parent are going your separate ways is likely to be the most significant news you have ever had to break to them.

How they initially outwardly react will have a lot to do with how they have seen you react to major news, but they may not know how to react, so be prepared for uncertainty, confusion and fear.

Questions, questions

As well as all those 'why?' questions, others you will be asked may include:

- Is this my fault?

- Are you cross with me?
- Are you cross with mum / dad?
- Where am I going to live now?
- Where's mum / dad going to live now?
- Where are the rest of us going to live now?
- Can we stay together?
- Will we have to move?
- Will we have to change schools?
- Where will all my things go?
- Can I tell my friends?
- What can / should I tell my friends?
- Doesn't mum / dad love me anymore?

How to answer

It may sound obvious but all of the above questions can be answered truthfully with love and understanding. As I said earlier, it's important to meet their questions head on and not avoid telling them what's going to happen now.

Protect them from hostilities

'My husband had a one-night stand while he was away with work. It was a massive shock and after he told me, he sunk into a depression. We were childhood sweethearts and have three children. Friends said I should leave him and tell the children what he had done. There was no way I was putting them through that while there was still a chance we could work at it. It was a very painful time. He went to stay with his mum and I had some time to think. I told him that I was going to fight for our marriage. The children were never told what was happening. Looking back, I'm glad about that.'

Jackie, mum to Chloe, Jack and Lauren.

It is important to maintain a sense of balance. Don't bad-mouth your partner. Have the compassion and dignity to allow your children not to be confronted with the nitty gritty of what has gone on at the heart of the relationship, and certainly never expect them to take sides.

Set your differences aside to allow your children the room to breathe, to gain an understanding of what is going to happen now, instead of dwelling on what has already gone on.

Questions may become a lot more complicated depending on the age of the child, some answers may just be too difficult for them to understand and some truthful responses may be inappropriate. Use your judgement and knowledge of your own children to allow you to know when this is the case.

But whatever you do, don't project any feelings of anger, resentment or

Blaming themselves

Children may view what's happening as a personal rejection that they have had a hand in.

Tell them:

- There is no need to blame themselves.
- They have not done anything to make this happen.
- You are not separating because they did anything naughty.
- You know how painful it is.
- You both still love them very much and always will.
- This happens to lots of families.
- You are there for them and so is the parent who is moving away.
- Nothing will stop you loving them.

Talking about emotions

Talking about how we feel can be hard for anyone, however old. To help children feel at ease and more ready to share their emotions, you should let them know that they have your full attention and must listen to them without interruptions or distractions. Tell them how pleased you are that they are able to talk to you and that what they say will not make you angry. You need to know how they feel.

Young children

'When I explained to my son, who was 10, that his dad and I were splitting up, I saw a real change in him; he began to turn into what he thought was a really good boy. He'd never been that naughty in the first place. He went to bed without question, whereas I'd usually have to keep asking him, and he started to jump up in the morning and offered to do his own breakfast. Bless him. It was lovely to see him making an effort but I was worried about him. When I spoke to him, he said that he felt sad for me and he didn't want to cause me any more upset. I told him that it was okay, he didn't make me sad by having to be asked to go to bed and he needed to think about himself as well as me.' Carol, mum to Alexander, 13.

Young children still depend very much on their parents and will find it hard to discuss how they feel. They may be angry – brace yourself for them blurting out that they 'hate' you, but don't take it to heart. This is a sign of the distress they are feeling.

Children aged from nine to 12 may have begun to forge important friendships and relationships outside the immediate close-knit circle of the family. They may find it easier to talk to you but can also be encouraged to talk to someone outside the home. Continue to invite their friends round and encourage them to see their friends as usual at different activities.

This is also the time to ask your children what they would like to happen now. If it's possible and appropriate, ask them which parent they would like to live with. It's also very important to protect them from grown-up worries and responsibilities.

'I really wanted mum and dad to stay together. I thought I was to blame and that if I had behaved better then dad would have been

They both tried to explain that this wasn't the case, that they found they had less and less to say to each other, but I couldn't understand. I thank God they were so patient and understanding with me.'

Philip, 20.

Teenagers

Teenagers may be less dependent on their family unit than younger siblings, but don't assume they will be less affected by the change in circumstances.

Teenagers may still feel angry about what has happened and this may be directed more at one parent than the other.

At this age, thoughts about their own relationships may start to figure in their minds. They may begin to question their own ability to maintain a long-term relationship. You need to reassure them that they have nothing to worry about, that your own relationship need have no effect on their present or future ones.

Temper outbursts

the context of everything your children are coming to terms with.

What else might they have to cope with?

What happens now?

Moving house may be on the horizon, as might a change in schools; that means more stress and more uncertainty.

Don'ts

- Whatever you do – don't expect your children to take sides.
- Don't use your children as a means of getting back at your partner.
- However hard it is, don't slate your partner.
- And never, ever expect your children to take on the role of your partner.

Outside help

Who else are your children close to?

The following may be able to offer help and support to your children and yourself:

- Grandparents.
- Family friends.
- Teachers.
- Family doctor.
- School counsellor.
- Youth group or activity leaders.
- Family counsellor.

There are also story books written for children of various ages which can help them see that they are not alone, and to help explain what is happening. The internet can also play a part in supplying further resources and help. See the help list and further reading for more information.

Action points

- Talk to teachers and youth leaders.
- Source any reading material suitable for your children's age group that could help them.
- Plan how to answer their questions.
- Tell them it's okay to be angry.

'Mattie went really quiet. I didn't know what to do. I bought a picture book about divorce, it really helped.'

David, dad to Matthew, four.

Summing Up

■ Do all you can to answer your children's questions, but don't include them in your hostilities.

■ Ease the guilt they feel.

■ Help them feel secure – maintain routine.

■ Seek outside help if needed.

Chapter Three

Red Tape and Legal Matters

The exception not the rule

You probably won't be surprised to learn that most families decide what happens now – where the children are going to live – between themselves.

In reality the dramatic courtroom scenes so beloved by soap screen writers only bear any relation to about one in 10 families – and I'd be willing to bet they are nowhere near as dramatic. Why is this? It's because parents have the best interests of their children at heart and a lengthy court procedure causes further upset. Separated parents who resort to the law to settle arguments over contact with their children risk making matters worse for all concerned.

Research published by the Joseph Rowntree Foundation in March 2004 contrasted the relative success of contact agreements reached by parents without legal intervention, with the stress placed on children after parents fail to agree or show lack of commitment to make arrangements.

The study suggested that lawyers rarely improve their clients' commitment to unwelcome contact arrangements and that applications for court orders tend to fuel conflict rather than resolve it.

It concluded that time and money spent trying to impose solutions through the courts would be better invested in services to improve relations between parents and children, helping them find their own solutions.

'Since applications for court orders appear to exacerbate rather than settle disputes, resources should be redirected towards more creative work to improve parental and parent-child relationships. Children too, should have greater access to counselling and other support.'

Liz Trinder, from the Joseph Rowntree Foundation.

'Our research
suggests that
provisions in
the Children
Act 1989,
encouraging
parents who
separate to
make workable
child contact

without external
intervention, are
fully justified.
But there are
major problems
with existing
procedures
for resolving
disputes and
imposing
arrangements
where no
agreement can
be reached.'
Liz Trinder, from the
Joseph Rowntree
Foundation.

Do it yourself

So ideally, all things being equal, and with you both wanting the best for your children and to cause them as little heartache as possible, you'll be able to agree with your former partner and children where they are going to live and how often they get to see each of you.

This shows your children that you can act like adults and you have their best interests at heart. While some parents may cling on to a belief that fighting for their kids shows how much they love them, an ability to put their needs first and being flexible shows a much greater commitment and maturity.

In fact, it may be a fear of not seeing your children as often as you would like that leads to courts getting involved.

sufficiently to make progress. As parents, you are in the best possible position to ensure your custody arrangements serve the specific needs of your family – that's for now and into the future.

Solving the potentially thorny questions of residency and access without the help of a legal system avoids a massive amount of stress for all involved, not to mention the associated costs. But such are the deep-running feelings that can cloud judgements at such an emotionally charged time; there may be no getting away from the fact that you are just not going to agree.

Nevertheless, you can do better than a court in deciding what is best for your children. You know your children better than a judge who has never met them before. Only if the children's safety or well-being is genuinely under threat and you cannot agree how to reduce the risk to them, can a court case be entirely necessary.

Why? Because it makes a bad situation worse, and what parent ever truly wants that for their children? No matter how much you reckon your life would improve if you got your desired outcome, the fact remains that children should ideally maintain contact with both parents.

Even if your former partner is apparently inflexible, or both parents want sole custody, then all is not lost. There's plenty of help available.

You will also need to improve your negotiation skills and may need some outside help. See chapter 8 for more information.

The next step: consider seeing a family counsellor

Relate counsellors can offer a variety of ways to help you and your former partner negotiate through your differences to find a compromise that is in all your interests. You may also have heard of mediation.

So what is it?

Mediation is not like counselling. It helps when you have decided to separate and deal positively with the imminent issues and practicalities. A mediator is a trained professional who will listen to the wishes of both parents.

If you still can't compromise for the sake of your children, mediation is the best option – and remains a million times better than toughing it out in court.

They can help with:

- Contact.
- Residence.
- Finances.
- Property.

If not now, when?

Even if mediation doesn't seem an option just now, don't rule it out altogether. Perhaps when feelings aren't running so high, you could make a go of it. If it doesn't work, that's when you have to consider court action.

'If I had my time again, I would have worked harder at family counselling. I needed my husband to see that he should be there for our son but he seemed to be on another planet – he was denying he had a new girlfriend but my friends had seen him with someone. The counsellor couldn't get much out of him, he seemed to dry up in the sessions.

'That just made me angry – for me and my son. I wanted to make him pay for what he had done to me, my son and our family. I can't believe we ended up going to court, it all got very messy. I never imagined that we would end up communicating through solicitors. We stopped it before it went too far and did manage to make arrangements in the end. Now my son sees his dad every week and he takes him to football training on a Sunday morning as well as on holiday with his new partner. I also have a new relationship now.

'Those weeks after we decided to split up were the hardest of my life – much harder than coming to the decision in the first place. It was such a grown-up step to take but looking back, I can't help feeling we behaved like children. I should have grabbed hold of my ex outside the family counselling sessions, shook him by the shoulders and said "we know we can't be together but let's make this work."'

Katie, mum to Simon, 14.

Going to court

Will I need a solicitor?

If you are heading for court, then you will need a solicitor. It's possible to get a free consultation with a solicitor who can help you work towards getting the best outcome for you and your children. There could be a difficult road ahead so make sure this trusted professional is someone that you like and can get on with.

Choosing the right solicitor also means you need to be confident that they are professionally qualified and properly regulated.

Faced with a large choice, you may not know where to turn. Ask family, friends and other contacts who they would recommend – word of mouth can count for a lot.

What is the court's role?

Family courts – and the law which guides them – examine parental responsibility, with the welfare of the child at the centre of all considerations, before deciding on what should happen next.

You should note that the terms 'custody' and 'access' which are still used in everyday speech, have been overtaken by 'residency' and 'contact' in the eyes of the law.

What are the laws affecting children in divorce?

Parental responsibility and the Children Act 1989

The Act says that the child's welfare is the most important consideration. It describes parental responsibility rather than the 'rights' of parents or children.

Mothers automatically have parental responsibility. However, if you were married when your child was born, both parents will have parental responsibility. If you are the father, and your child was born after 1st December 2003, and you are named on the birth certificate, you will also have automatic parental responsibility.

What does parental responsibility mean?

This refers to the rights, duties and responsibilities associated with being a parent. It means you are responsible for the following concerning your child:

- Protecting.
- Maintaining their upkeep.
- Naming.
- Choosing a school and making sure it's attended.

- Ensuring medical attention when needed.

- Appointing a guardian in the event of your death.

- Applying for a passport.

- Representing the child.

- Deciding where to live.

- Choosing a religion.

What about financial responsibility?

A parent has financial responsibility until a child is 17, or leaves full-time education.

If I don't see my child, do I still have to pay?

The father or mother is obliged to pay for this support whether or not there is any contact. The two issues should be completely separate but, sadly, falling out about maintenance payments can lead to disputes over contact. However, a parent who has regular contact is far more likely to keep up regular payments. You should attempt to keep these two crucial issues separate at all times – don't let your feelings about one influence the other.

So what do the courts actually do?

They make decisions about the future of the child or children. They do this with guidance from the Children Act, stressing the child's welfare.

What do they take into account?

- What the child wants.

- His or her needs – physical, emotional and educational.

- Predicted effects of a change in circumstances.

As well as this, the court also examines any other details about the parents' relationship that they consider relevant and how capable they consider each parent is of meeting the needs just outlined; in other words, how capable is each parent of meeting the child's needs?

What is the court aiming for?

Going to court is another step to resolving the future for the best benefit to your children.

It's not a means of settling any other arguments you may have with your former partner or asking a court to take sides. It is not a power battle as portrayed in those soap operas mentioned earlier.

Think of your children throughout all of this. They will be hoping for an amicable solution that you can all stick to.

What will the outcome be?

If a residence order is made, then there will almost certainly be a contact order made in respect of the other parent.

If it is contact rather than residence that is being contested, then the resulting order will concentrate on details of future contact, how often it should take place and whether it should be face to face.

Whatever the detail of the order, it is likely to be temporary so that parents can work towards resolving the problems that led to the order being sought.

Where can I find out more?

The Children and Family Court Advisory and Support Service (CAFCASS) website (www.cafcass.gov.uk) is an excellent information guide for all members of the family.

CAFCASS looks after the interests of children involved in family proceedings, working with families to advise on what it considers to be in the children's best interests.

'Contact arrangements should focus primarily on the welfare and interests of the children involved who can often get caught in the crossfire of parental conflict. This research provides practical suggestions to help families make workable contact arrangements for their children.'

Jonathan Tross, CAFCASS Chief Executive.

What should I tell my children about the court case?

Ensure you explain as much as you can about why you are going to court: because mum and dad both love them very much and are trying to find a way of doing what's best for them.

Don't ask them to take messages for you, or to report back on what their other parent has been saying – you should not expect them to keep secrets or negotiate with your former partner.

Did you know?

Most family court proceedings are held in private; the media is not allowed in and the decisions are usually not made public.

Even on reaching adulthood, children whose lives have been changed by a decision are not always able to discover what the court ordered and why. This has led to a feeling that family courts operate in secret and are unaccountable.

The government has outlined plans to open up family courts to the media – provided individuals involved in the case remain anonymous.

Action points

▪ Find out about Relate in your area. Visit www.relate.org.uk.

▪ Learn more about CAFCASS and the support it provides.

Summing Up

An amicable solution between separated parents is the best outcome. Even if this can't be achieved by the parents themselves, counselling or mediation may help. Court action is a last resort.

Chapter Four

What Children Want

You may not consider *The Parent Trap*, *Mrs Doubtfire* or *Adrian Mole* to be the most realistic pieces of fiction. But one aspect of these popular comic works does ring true, and that's the children wanting to see their parents back together.

Unfortunately in real life, the heartbreak behind such a secret mission to reunite parents is not so entertaining. Whilst there may be a happy ending, it may not be the one they long for.

Children may confide in you that this is what they are hoping for, they may just tell their friends or they may keep it to themselves. Whatever happens, you need to take these feelings seriously, don't dismiss them too quickly. Take time to explain clearly and fully that in your case this isn't going to happen, but they are not alone.

How is life going to change?

There are going to be changes that have an impact practically, emotionally and financially. These are huge concepts for children to get to grips with, so you need to be with them every tentative step of the way, making sure you can do all that you can to help them.

There may be hurdles and obstacles along the way, there may be issues connected with jealousy, bitterness, blame and resentment. But whatever has caused such issues, this is not a conversation to have with your children. Look forward and help them look forward too.

Watch out for changes in behaviour; look out for moodiness, sleep problems or temper tantrums. If you begin to worry that your children may be depressed, then seek help and support from your family doctor. Talk to your children about how they feel and above all, be there for them. See chapter 8 for more on how a family doctor can help and why you need not fear going to see them.

Clarity: stick to the facts

- Do not kid yourself that telling your children that mum and dad no longer love each other is enough. They need to know more than this. However, they don't need to know all the details.

- Stick to the facts and don't bring blame or bitterness into it. Regardless of whoever initiated the split, it is now a joint decision and should be portrayed to your children as such.

- Continue to give your children plenty of opportunities to talk so they know their feelings matter.

- Do fun things together and continue to keep your promises, just like you did before the split.

- Try to minimise the upheaval caused by the separation, and let them know that it's okay to still love the two of you.

- If possible, maintain their contact with the extended family of your former partner. Their relationships with grandparents, uncles, aunties and cousins can still be nurtured.

- Don't talk about any concerns you have with your former partner in front of your children.

- Carry on with the usual activities and routines, whenever possible.

- Make time to sit with them, to play with them, to watch them.

- At all costs, try to stay calm while you are around them; shouting only encourages them to shout.

Family loyalty

Children are extremely loyal to both their parents, whatever the situation. They may deny or hide their own feelings for fear of upsetting one or the other, but this means that they may say one thing to your former partner and another to you.

Tell them that it's okay to be honest. They don't have to tell both parents that they want to live with them. Make sure they really understand that this isn't possible – choosing between their parents may be a mountain they don't want to climb.

This becomes even more important when your children are hoping you will get back together. It's perfectly understandable and natural for children to feel this way, so don't get frustrated with them and speak out against their faithfulness to your former partner – whatever you feel that partner is guilty of.

Easing their guilt

Children may feel guilty that a separation is on the horizon. They may believe that they could have done something to prevent this, and will need to understand that the divorce or separation stems from long-held problems between the parents, and has not been influenced by them in any way, shape or form.

Don't encourage them to feel guilty and don't make them feel bad for still loving their other parent. The key point is to let them know that it's still okay to want to spend time with both of you – tell them that you understand and that they are encouraged to do so.

Tell them often and clearly that the break-up is not their fault. Constantly reinforce this message to help it sink in. As adults we need that constant reinforcement in our home and working lives. Why would a child be any different? Of course they need more reassurance, so don't ever think that telling them once and thinking they can move on will be enough.

When there has been an affair

Children want their mum and dad back together, so their feelings towards the parent who has had an affair may be more difficult. If there is a new partner waiting in the wings then children need to know and be involved in discussions about what happens next. If they don't, they will remain suspicious and will not fully understand what is happening. This suspicion can also grow into resentment.

Get these feelings out into the open; discuss them as honestly and fully as you can. Think about how they will view a new partner if the affair turns into a more

mum and dad's relationship?

Just because you love your new partner, it doesn't necessarily follow that your children will. Reassure them that they have all the time in the world to adjust and that they are still what matters most in your life. It will be important to tell them that this new person is not taking the place of their mum or dad.

Security

Despite initial reservations and difficult feelings around the arrival of a new partner, most children will want things to settle down and to get on with the new adult in their lives as time goes on.

At the same time they will still want to see their other parent as often as they can and to be not only allowed, but encouraged to have a good time. You shouldn't pick over the details of what they have done whilst away from you and criticise your former partner's parenting skills. Children want their parents to be friends, whoever else is on the scene.

Agree to rules, routines and roles for this stage of all your lives and stick to them, casting aside any previous bitterness or resentment. Do all you can to get on in front of your children, not only with your former partner but also their new partner. More information on this is provided in chapter 6.

Don't share details of the divorce

Children don't want or need to know all about court matters or contentious financial issues that have accompanied the break-up.

Don't argue in front of them

- Don't play out any conflicts either in front of them or so that they can hear on the phone.
- Be polite to your former partner.
- Don't bad-mouth their other parent – either for how they act now or have done in the past.

However hard it seems, strive to develop an amicable relationship with your former partner and to maintain it.

Money worries

If your circumstances now dictate that money is tighter, it's easy to believe that this will be a major blow to your relationship with your children.

But while a reduced family budget may have all sorts of practical implications, don't ever lose sight of the fact that what a child needs more than anything is your love. And you still have that in spades!

Look after yourself

Your children want to see you happy, looking well and relaxed. How can you care for them properly if you aren't caring for yourself?

- Keep in touch with friends; don't shut yourself away.
- Find new friends and interests.
- Take care of your health and your children's health. Don't put yourself last.
- Eat sensibly and find time to exercise.

'I hated it when dad went on about how mum had let herself go. I spoke up for her when I could, but it turned into every little thing – mum used to look better, used to do this better or that. I told dad I couldn't come and see him so often if he was going to spoil it by going on about mum all the time. It just made me sad. '

Bonnie, 15.

Special days and holidays

If you no longer have a close relationship with your former partner's family, then children may feel that holidays such as Christmas and special days such as birthdays may not hold as much appeal.

Put yourself in their shoes. They may have fewer presents and they may have fewer people to invite to their party. If your former partner's relatives do come, there may be an uncomfortable atmosphere.

All of these things make it difficult, but you have to do all you can to keep these

Again, if money is less plentiful than it was, don't make the mistake of thinking that special means expensive.

Find new ways of spending time together and new activities that are free or cost little. Take advantage of special offers or discounts advertised in the media or negotiated by support groups.

Holidays

What are you going to do about going on holiday? When can you go with your children and when can your former partner?

You may want to alternate. For example, if you celebrate Christmas one of you could have the children one year, and one of you will have the children the next time.

Your children's wishes should be paramount. If they want to go with your former partner, do not take this as a reflection on you or your parenting skills. Encourage them to go and have a good time. Share in their excitement and don't make them feel they can't reminisce when they get back.

Above all, you should endeavour to make your children as happy as possible throughout all of these arrangements.

'I stayed in an unhappy marriage for years for our know when it happened that the divorce did hurt him, but we talked and talked and talked about what he wanted so that I could help him continue to feel happy, secure and loved.'

Robert, dad to Jason, 13.

Action points

- Keep in touch with friends.
- Get yourself a health check.
- Find time for you.
- Plan what will happen during holidays.

Summing Up

- Your children will want you to get back together.
- Don't bad-mouth your former partner in front of them.
- Let them keep in touch with their grandparents if at all possible.
- Help your children feel secure.
- Remember money doesn't buy you love.

Chapter Five

Maintaining Contact

Separation is a process – not an event

Think about it. Separation and divorce go on for years. We have already established that it's not the separation itself which can be the all-singing, all-dancing bolt from the blue that has an everlasting effect on your children's happiness, but the way it is handled.

The major part of this is the time after the news has been broken, as everyone involved adapts to their changing circumstances. If parents engrossed in a conflict with their former partner during this sensitive time can call a truce and stick to it – for the sake of their children – they will reap the benefits.

That time following the actual parting of the ways involves plentiful life changes. Some will be obvious, important changes that will take a lot of getting used to – from who lives where and with whom, to how often the children can get together with their parent who no longer lives with them. But just as important are the changes the children are going through as they continue to grow.

You can't seek to cope with these obvious changes without also taking these more subtle changes and growing pains into account.

How you set off on the road of organising when and how your children stay with or see each of you will have as great an effect on their stability, outlook and moods as how you broke the news that you were splitting up.

Arrangements for contact among divorced or separated parents are as diverse as the families themselves. You can only do your best in the circumstances. Be kind to yourself, keep communication open as much as possible and put the children's well-being and stability at the heart of your plans.

There are going to be lots of changes that you will have to deal with that shouldn't concern your children, some bigger than others. Help them understand what is happening and why.

More contact equals less arguing!

At first glance, this may seem a confusing statement, but a study in 2002 by the Joseph Rowntree Foundation revealed that out of the families interviewed where contact was working, the conflict between parents was

This does not mean there were no problems at all – that would be pie in the sky – but it was felt that the benefits of contact outweighed the problems.

'However hard it seems, strive to develop an amicable relationship with your ex and to maintain it.'

Where do you need to work at it?

Problems identified by the researchers, which caused stress for children, included:

- Difficulties with new partners (see chapter 6 for more on step-families).
- Contact didn't work either through a lack of commitment by parents, or because of the conflict caused.
- Parents were, or grew, ambivalent about the importance of contact.
- Disagreements arose about the form or amount of contact.
- Children believed that they hadn't been adequately consulted about arrangements.

Where contact was working best, the parents had managed to maintain an amicable relationship, at least in front of the children, despite some inevitable tension.

Money worries come into the equation here. If you have lost a wage earner from your household, then the remaining budget available needs to go further. When matters concerning maintenance payments rear their head, it can be hard to see a way out. One thing that experts agree you shouldn't do is turn arguments about cash into arguments about access. This will only lead to greater resentment.

The household contents also need to be fairly divided, with children's feelings being taken into account. More than anything, they need to continue to feel 'at home', to feel secure and loved. Anything you can do to ease this process by allowing their regular routines to continue will help. Also how and where favourite items are kept or moved has a large part to play.

Making contact work

According to the researchers, there were two main factors leading to the success of the contact arrangements. These were a commitment from both parents and a 'role bargain'.

That means that the parents were clearly dedicated to working together despite their history and differences. They had accepted their roles within the new family set-up and didn't exacerbate the situation by harking back to any objections as to who was the resident parent and who was the non-resident.

Let your children enjoy contact with your former partner

Why waste energy and cloud their minds by passing on resentment about their mum or dad? It sounds simple, doesn't it?

Actively helping your children to see their other parent and encouraging them to spend time away from you is key and helps strengthen contact arrangements. You know your former partner isn't perfect. Nor are you. In these situations, say the researchers, parents are doing the best they can for the sake of their children.

Who can do any more than that? Recognise your own strengths and weaknesses and learn to compromise. Why? Because who can fight forever? And who wants their children to see them fighting forever?

Life is not black and white. So why, unless your children are in danger, should you paint your former partner like that? The most important thing you can do is compromise – to allow your children to grow up surrounded by all the love they can get, as much as circumstances allow. If you want happy children, be nice about, and to, your former partner.

Wherever possible you need to be as flexible as possible, allowing your

their grandparents will only add to the enormous amount of feelings they are experiencing. In every decision you make about what happens now, do your utmost to show that their needs are upper most in your mind.

Helping your children adjust to two homes

Children's sense of security comes from routine, familiarity and predictability. That means that a family way of doing things, rules, conventions and discipline remain vital in helping children feel secure.

It's important, however tempting it is, not to undermine the rules laid down by your former partner. Talk about what is and isn't allowed, agree limits, boundaries and, where necessary, punishments.

On a practical level this means that children may only be allowed to play on their computer games, games consoles or watch DVDs for a given time in a week – whichever parent they are with. There may be set times for doing homework, household chores or relaxing together.

If these times were acceptable to you and your children beforehand, then there's no reason to change them now and you certainly shouldn't fall into a trap of allowing them more treats in the hope of swaying their loyalty or expecting them to side with you.

'Children's sense of security comes from routine, familiarity and predictability. That means that a family way of doing things, rules, conventions and discipline remain vital in helping children feel secure.'

A sense of where is home is paramount

Having to divide their time between two homes will mean your children could feel anxious and insecure. You should listen to their concerns and help them adjust as best you can. If they uncharacteristically misbehave during this time, don't jump to conclusions about the reasons behind their misbehaviour.

Below is some advice that will help:

- Be as patient and loving as you can. Give them time to adjust. Don't expect them to feel at ease too quickly.

- Be consistent and reliable. Show that family routines are still in place where possible and don't overindulge your children because you feel guilty for the disruption caused to their lives.

- Help the transition by enabling them to have their stuff at both homes to give them an added bit of familiarity.

- Some parents try using their children as a messenger. 'Tell your dad you shouldn't be watching that programme, it's too old for you' or 'Ask your mother if she can please stop picking you up early.' Don't do it. It's very upsetting to be caught in the middle.

Stay in touch: don't divorce the children!

If your former partner moves away from the area, do all you can to ensure your children can still speak on the phone, communicate by email or social networking sites and plan visits during school holidays.

It has never been easier to keep in touch. Your children may have MySpace, Bebo or Facebook sites. Ask them if you can link up too – what could be easier when you are not physically around?

Simply knowing that their parents still love them, and that they are acting as parents even though they are far away, can have a major effect on children's frame of mind, well-being and confidence. Regular letters, postcards, notes and emails can all help in strengthening a relationship that began the day they were born.

Time between homes can be split to best suit all involved.

Take into account:

- How to achieve minimum disruption.
- What the children prefer, however difficult this is.
- ~~How often and for how long you or your partner are at work – don't 'ever~~
- How far away the homes are.
- Can they continue to see their friends?
- How draining it can be to live out of a suitcase.
- The need to be kept informed of where the children are.

Concern over the continuing role of the father

'I remember reading about Bob Geldof and his campaign to help dads who couldn't see their children as much as they wanted. I thought, that'll never happen to me, but it did. I have lovely, happy times with my daughter, even if she is just at my house and invites her friends round. But when she goes back to her mum, I do get upset. It's the worst thing ever. I would never have wanted to be a "weekend dad" and needed to find someone to talk to about this. I found an online forum and that helped. I don't go on so much now but it still feels weird as a bloke to discuss your feelings. I wish I could talk to her mum more, but she doesn't want to know really.'
Kevin, dad to Lauren, 14.

Whatever has led to the separation, there's no doubt that dads who don't see their children as much as they would like, suffer great amounts of anguish and grief.

Read any popular newspaper and it won't be long before you stumble across a story recounting the pain of the dads who feel they have been forced out of their children's lives or don't see them enough. A faltering relationship between separated parents undoubtedly adds to the problems.

The quality of relationships between parents and children and between parents themselves is important in helping children adjust to life after separation. Children should also be informed of what's going on.

Fathers may face extra difficulties in organising contact when they have long or irregular working hours or accommodation that is not suitable for extended visits. Providing sufficient space to allow both parents to offer reasonable comfort on overnight stays for the children requires considerable resources.

Families Need Fathers (FNF) is a charity providing information and support on shared parenting issues arising from family breakdown. It also gives support to divorced and separated parents, irrespective of gender or marital status. Their primary concern is the maintenance of the child's relationship with both parents.

Founded in 1974, FNF helps thousands of parents every year. FNF has been supportive of recent work by the Equal Opportunities Commission, especially recent work examining the family.

John Baker, from FNF says: 'One of the barriers to the equality of women in employment, politics and the like has been the expectation that childcare is solely or mainly the responsibility of the children's mother. The wish of fathers to have more of a role here has been growing rapidly but has had little encouragement from public policy. They have been denied access to the emotionally richest part of life. The EOC has drawn attention to this issue. We pledge ourselves to continue this aspect of its work.

'One of the most extreme examples of discrimination occurs after family separation. It is assumed that when this happens one parent, most often the mother, must take on virtually all of the parenting. The other, most often the father, is expected to finance this, but to become an occasional visitor to the children. The most important people to suffer from this policy are the children.'

FNF also believe that 'Shared parenting helps with the emotional loss of children and parents. It also helps reduce poverty, reduces behaviour that causes personal and social problems, improves health, education and work performance. It promotes social inclusion, the safety of children and reduces domestic violence. It improves family relationships and parenting in the next generation.

'Founded in 1974, FNF helps thousands of parents every year. FNF has been supportive of recent work by the Equal Opportunities Commission, especially recent work examining the family.'

'The solution to these problems requires strategies across the whole of public policy. If the courts ensured that children had both parents involved in their lives, the benefit to society would follow. Our current "parenting deficit" and many of the associated personal and social problems would rapidly diminish.'

After divorce or separation fathers have to establish a new role, one distinctly separate from that of mothers. The amount and frequency of the contact they existent, and contact with children infrequent, there are few, if any, other means open to them for sustaining and supporting an active role in their children's lives.

FNF research shows that post-divorce fatherhood is far from easy or straightforward – love is most certainly not enough. They say that it's essential that post-divorce parenting is acknowledged as the difficult, challenging role it is.

Asked in their experience and the experience of families they have been able to offer support to, what the main problems are that children face when their parents split, Nick Barnard from FNF says that parents 'using' children in disputes with their former partners is all too usual.

He says: 'Whilst our work is focused on ensuring parents are able to fulfil their parental responsibilities, a common element of separation is for parents to involve children in their own personal disagreements – using the children "as a weapon" in the arguments. Needless to say that this can be catastrophic for a child's welfare and should be avoided at all costs.'

So what are the obstacles to harmony in a new relationship, involving children after divorce or separation? How realistic is it to think that they can be overcome? How realistic is it to expect parents to work together to try to put the children first? What steps can the adults in these relationships take to help their children?

Nick says: 'FNF is above all a child-focused organisation and we would urge all separating parents to remain so as well. It is not a question of being realistic, but of being absolutely paramount and necessary that parents, no matter what their internal disputes may be, put the children, for whom they are mutually responsible, first.

'FNF accepts that divorce and separation are facts of life, and that sometimes there will be circumstances where a separation is best for all parties. Our core belief remains that children have a right to a sustained loving relationship with both their parents and to remove the significant presence of one will have negative consequences for them. Research has consistently shown that children who have a significant relationship with both parents have a lower chance of coming to harm. Whether this contact is with parents who are together or separated is often beyond our control – what is within our control is to ensure that it does always happen.

Don't try to buy your children's love

There may be a temptation to spoil your children with material things – trips out, presents, sweets – you name it. Don't give in. Your time, love and respect are worth a whole lot more.

Have fun

Yes really. None of us can stay angry, confused or upset forever. Have a laugh and let your children be children. Do your best to take them out for a variety of family activities, away from it all. This needn't be expensive – go somewhere new and try something different. What's stopping you? You can still create happy memories.

'The days and weeks immediately after we told Alfie that daddy was moving out, were the hardest. But there was still some laughter. One day I sat him down and asked what he wanted to do now…When he looked up at me with his big eyes, shrugged his shoulders and told me that he wanted to go to the new ice skating rink, I had to laugh. I jumped up and gave him a cuddle and off we went.'

Dea, mum to Alfie, nine.

Action points

▪ Find some activities you can enjoy with your children, set a realistic date to go and do them.

▪ Research Families Need Fathers, Relate and other helpful organisations. (See help list .)

'**If any parent, no matter what stage of a separation or divorce they may be at and whatever the related circumstances, feels they would benefit from assistance in order to increase and improve contact with their children, Families Need Fathers is always here to assist.**'
Nick Barnard, FNF.

Summing Up

- Work hard to make contact arrangements as agreeable as possible for all involved.
- Remember children need both their parents.

- Maintain contact by keeping in touch, no matter how far away you are.

Chapter Six

Step-families

'I definitely had unrealistic expectations when we moved in with Dave. I thought he would love my son and daughter like his own from day one. But he didn't know them like I did and was quite nervous around them. I didn't see that coming. He doesn't have children and was scared of saying no to them as he thought this would turn them against him. I had to explain that this wasn't so. We talked about how discipline could work and how awkward he felt. Things have improved as he has got to know them better, but it was a shaky start.'

Eleanor, mum to Bethany, seven, and Jake, 11.

Oh no, mum and dad are dating again

At an age where children may not have thought about their own sexuality, or are coming to terms with it, having to get to grips with the fact that one or both parents are seeing new people can be quite a hurdle.

In some families, a new relationship may have started before the separation, or may begin soon after. Elsewhere, the parents may not feel right or confident about dating for months or years. They may simply not have the time. Whatever the situation, seeing your mum or dad date will trigger a gamut of feelings that are strange and possibly frightening for a child.

That's why it's important for you not to expect your children to adapt too quickly. Take things as slowly as you can and hang on in there. This is possibly the biggest change of all for the whole family to get used to.

It's not something that your children have chosen and they may not share your optimism about what's going to happen now. Like it or not, the new person will be seen as a stranger by your children and you will have to work hard to take their feelings into account as to how and when your new partner becomes more of an integral part of the family.

Inevitably, your children won't want to see you get hurt. On a more practical

person becomes a more permanent fixture, resentment may build.

How all of this affects your children can be influenced every step of the way by your explanations and actions in helping them adapt – but don't expect miracles. If one parent has left a marriage or long-term relationship for someone else, then they are going to have to consider the emergence of feelings of betrayal and anger.

You should provide your children with realistic opportunities to voice their feelings – whether it is you or your former partner that has brought about this change. Encourage your children not to bottle up their feelings but to let them out – however worried they are that voicing them will cause further upset. They have to understand that their needs and feelings are being taken into account.

These may be very difficult things to hear, forcing you to confront again all the heartache that has gone into the decision to split, but your children deserve to be heard. There may also be jealousy, confusion and guilt.

When new relationships get serious

The number of second and third marriages goes up each year, which means so does the number of step-families. It can be very difficult for step-parents and step-children to adjust to and live with each other, so it's crucial to communicate well and to know when to compromise.

Seeing your parents move on to a new long-term partner is one of the most pressing issues affecting children whose parents part.

These days children are more likely to have friends who have also been through this transition, and they can be encouraged to talk to them about what's to be expected.

Your children need to know about the new partner and what this means for their future. Don't think it would be a wise move, for example, to surprise them with the news, thinking that they will be delighted for you. They won't be.

One of the worst things you can do is attempt to shield your children's feelings by not telling them about the new person in your life. That's a recipe for more hurt and mistrust as they think things are happening behind their backs.

If they haven't taken well to you dating, you can be sure they aren't going to be enthusiastic about adjusting to their new family arrangement. It's a final blow for any hopes they were harbouring to bring their parents back together. The fairytale ending is lost and a new mythical stereotype enters the picture – a step-parent. Don't forget, there is also the prospect of step-siblings.

According to ChildLine, worries that children have about step-families include:

- The difficulty of getting to know lots of new people at once.
- Challenges of having a new parent imposing discipline or rules.
- Seeing their mum or dad change when they are around the new partner.
- Worries about how much their parents love their step-children compared to them.

Your children may find it difficult to accept all these changes. Wouldn't you if you had no say in them? The arrival of a new baby into the relationship can also prove a difficult time for them, but they will adapt.

How well and how quickly is down to you.

You should:

- Stress an understanding that a step-parent doesn't take the place of their other parent.
- Help them endeavour to build a unique, balanced and positive relationship with the step-parent.
- Encourage them not to take sides against their step-parent with your former partner.
- Encourage your new partner to be patient and understanding.
- Stress the importance of not criticising your former partner to your new partner.

'Seeing your parents move on to a new long-term partner is one of the most pressing issues affecting children whose parents part. If they haven't taken well to you dating, you can be sure they aren't going to be enthusiastic about adjusting to their new family arrangement.'

- Avoid arguments over parenting methods.

- Discuss with your new partner differences in parenting styles or discipline away from your children.

- Help your children understand that your situation is not unique and that there is a growing trend towards step-families.

- Your children need to know where they stand. Explain fully the role their step-parent is going to play in their lives.

Of course this is a new relationship for all of you. Take each day as it comes and don't be hard on yourself when things don't go to plan.

All families have problems. You should expect them. Be good humoured and patient as you chart these new waters together.

What can I tell younger children?

You should explain that when parents separate and then live away from each other, it's normal that they then see new people. New friends can turn into a boyfriend or girlfriend. They want a chance to love you too.

Your children have nothing to be scared of because of this. Just because you love a new person, it doesn't mean you love your children any less. Choose your words carefully. Use terms that can be easily understood. Are you sure what you are planning to say, really is that easy to grasp?

What about money?

Consider the financial implications of starting out as a step-family. Budget as well as you can. There are more people in the equation now, so you must understand your new partner's approach to money and how this fits in with your children's expectations.

Explain to your children that you are taking things one step at a time.

> 'I like being step-family. It has opened my mind and prepared me for other things life can throw at me. I think step-families get a bad press. Children in all families face different problems, issues and challenges. What makes us so different?'
>
> Jonathan, 16.

Action points

- Explain to your children that they are not alone – there are more than 2.5 million step-families in the UK.
- Take time to plan with your new partner about how to explain things to your children.
- Agree on important issues about contact with your former partner.
- Allow your new partner's relationship with your children to develop over time.

'When I met Angela, it was very difficult at first. I didn't like her. I blamed her for splitting my mum and dad up. I knew we would never be the best of friends. I suppose I'm used to her now, as she is still with my dad but I don't mind admitting I get jealous of the attention she gets from my dad.'

Michelle, 17.

Summing Up

- Children have serious worries about step-families.
- But they can be very resilient and can adapt.
- Take one day at a time.

Chapter Seven

Teenage and Adult Children

It's easy to assume that the older the child, the lesser the impact of their parents' separation.

'They're not children, they'll be fine,' we say and on we go. They may even be expected to support their parent through this difficult time, rather than the other way around. However, teenage or adult children can be hit hardest of all, so it's important not to dismiss their fears and concerns.

Recent studies and a blaze of publicity have reported that adult children of divorce may have trouble finding a partner as they are less likely to want to create problems for their own children.

Relate counsellor Mo Kurimbokus, says that whatever the age of the child, the news that their parents are separating is likely to be a blow. Openness, honesty and good communication skills are key in working towards the future.

It's just as important to listen to older children about how they feel and what they want as it is the younger ones, he says. But while the hurt felt may be the same, it can manifest itself in different ways.

However, older children may prove harder to talk to. While a younger child may not question that they are still loved and aren't to blame, parents of older children may find themselves on the receiving end of blame for wrecking a family.

Parents should remember that the older the child, the more likely they are to feel their loyalty is being tested. An older child would be made more aware of some of the details of the break-up and may feel they want to take sides, says Dr Kurimbokus.

'Older children can make judgements about their parents introducing new people. What if an elder child doesn't get on with a new partner? That can lead to complications.

'For example, they may blame their dad for starting a relationship with "that woman." But the parent has to explain that while the relationship with the other parent has changed, the relationship with their child hasn't and isn't going to.

Dr Kurimbokus advises parents to work together, while considering the potential anger from the children and to be there for them. And he stresses that in some circumstances, it is possible that the break-up could come as a relief.

'If there has been a lot of rows, or if there has been violence then the separation may be a relief for the children. There are cases where a father will say that they see more of their children after a divorce than they did before.

'Honesty and openness are important. Parents of older children, just like those of any age, have to work together and let them know that they are loved as before and are not to blame for what has happened.'

What has happened so far?

Chances are that your teenager may have already witnessed or felt the fallout from a strained relationship, so the news that you are going to separate may not be a bolt out of the blue for them. Don't be surprised when they tell you they knew something was up and that they feared this would be the outcome.

Adding to this with the finer details of what has caused the separation may be hard for them. You must make sure you don't confuse or upset them with accusations about your former partner or say anything that could make them feel they are forced to take sides.

That said, it is important to answer their questions with integrity and respect for their feelings. Find a way of doing this that doesn't influence negative feelings about their other parent.

A sense of loss

Even if you have moved away from a secure family environment with two parents in it, being split up can be a devastating blow.

It can throw up new questions and feelings about their childhood as they wonder about their parents' relationship back then. Now more than ever, they are confronted with the realisation that their parents aren't, and never have been, perfect.

How might they react?

Teenagers whose parents separate have been reported to:

- Feel rejected.

- Get angry.

- Grow depressed.

- Become disillusioned with relationships.

- Show signs of more disruptive behaviour.

There is an added difficulty that you may already be aware of – teenagers are already coping, in many cases, with complex emotions that stir up such behaviour. How do you know this is caused by the separation?

The important thing is to remember that erratic behaviour is normal. Muster all your emotional resources to be there for them.

They may appear to want to reject you – perhaps they are embarrassed by what has happened and don't want to rock the boat with their image to their friends.

Perhaps, on top of the usual trials and tribulations of being a teenager, coping with news of their parents splitting up may cause extra problems. Everyone will be different. There's no point expecting the worst but be prepared for the fallout nevertheless.

Another possible turn of events for the parent of a teenager at this difficult time is to find themselves on the receiving end of an accusatory tirade based on what they think is and isn't the right way to behave. A teenager may appear to make their mind up about the rights and wrongs of the situation in the blink of an eye and have no qualms about making their opinion clear.

Try to take their snap judgment in your stride. You know them better than

In this situation, space is needed. Let them go to their room, let them play their music at full blast if they want.

Help them come to terms with the fact that while they may be older than other brothers or sisters, it's okay to suddenly feel more like a child, even though they are expected to get more of a grasp of the situation.

Your teenage child – not a shoulder to cry on

'I hated the way my mum and dad seemed to suddenly treat me like an adult when it suited them. I didn't want to know about the details of their rows. I found that quite painful. If I had been younger, there's no way they would have thought they could include me in on that. I don't know what they were thinking. It was as if they had thought I was old enough to be involved in this great big mess. But I wanted my mum and dad! I don't mind admitting that. I felt bewildered.'
Adam, 16.

With all of those emotions bubbling under the surface, it's important that you assess the boundaries of your relationship with your teenage child. That means, don't treat them like someone they're not. They are still your child and as such you should be there for them – not them for you.

Assure them that they aren't to blame for the break-up, and remain as you were – don't try and be both mum and dad to them but continue in the role they already know and love. They won't expect anything different.

At the same time, don't expect them to step in to the shoes of your former partner, to take on their roles and responsibilities because they are the oldest – even if they say they would like to. Work together to ensure chores or tasks done by your former partner are shared out fairly. Your teenage child should not be your confidante, expected to take sides or judge their other parent's behaviour.

Just like younger children, they don't need to know about all of the transgressions by the other parent. Why would they? You have both been role models for them up until now, so kicking the pedestal away will be hard to bear. Nor should they be called upon to be a messenger or go-between.

You wouldn't dream of burdening a younger child with such a blurring of the lines between parent and child, so don't think it's fitting with an older child either.

Be there for them – to listen. Try not to allow them to bottle up their feelings, which may cause problem behaviour, now or in the future. Try to reduce the changes they'll have to take on board – if it is possible, don't change schools and don't make them give up the activities they enjoy.

You need to help them understand that things will get better – teenagers should grasp this more than younger siblings. Help them appreciate that the whole family is affected by the changes taking place and encourage them to work with you to build for future happiness.

Finally, you should explain that separation can be for the best. Who wants to live with squabbling parents or moody parents who are suppressing their resentment?

The lead up to a separation puts a strain on everyone. Endeavouring to make things work as well as researching sources of outside support for your teenagers can help you all come to terms with what's happening.

What if they don't want to talk?

When a teenager finds out that their parents are splitting up, they are likely to feel embarrassed. What their friends think of them is very important. They don't want to be the odd one out – they don't mind being talked about but want it to be for the right reasons!

'My parents had been rowing for ages, but we didn't know why. It was horrible. When they told me and my sister they were separating it was still a shock but a relief too in a funny sort of way. I'm much happier now I can see mum is happier too.'

Chrissie, 14.

If they would rather confide in friends than you, then accept this and allow them the freedom to do so. At the same time, be there for them, for the times they do want to talk.

What if it's 'all about them?'

and what happens now will include questions about who is going to drive them to band practice, take them to gymnastics or give them pocket money.

You can be prepared for these questions as you know your own circumstances better than anyone else. If they lash out and say that they are suffering because of something that isn't their fault then you have to ride the storm. Wouldn't you have felt the same at their age?

Adults feel abandoned and alone

What happens when everything you grew up believing in starts to fall apart? Does this sound like an exaggeration to you? To an adult who finds out their parents are going to split up, it's anything but.

The biggest mistake you can make when considering the effect of a divorce or separation on your older or adult children is to assume because they are all grown up, they can take it in their stride.

They may feel that nobody understands – that while there appears to be a support network in place for younger children, meanwhile the expectation is that older children can 'just get on with it'.

They may feel abandoned, as if nobody cares about them as they attempt to continue to care for their own families, or alone. Who on earth can help them? Answer: you can.

If you have adult children, it is also important to help ease their isolation through frank discussions. While feeling the pain of the separation, they may feel that nobody will understand because of their age, urging them to 'pull themselves together' instead.

They will want and need to keep out of the arguments that characterise the split, yet they are often sucked into the fray. Don't say to them one minute, 'It's not your fault, we both love you,' then undo your good work with accusations about what has led to the break-up. You may think the other parent is a louse for the way they have treated you, but your children shouldn't be encouraged to share this view.

You should help them stay out of it. If you call on them for support, they won't be able to refuse. Is it really fair to put them in this position? Don't ask their opinion on what has happened or ask them to see your side, don't seek to have the same sort of intimate conversations with them as you would with a close friend. Ring that friend instead! Just as your older child doesn't want to hear about their parents' sex life, or lack of it, nor do they want to hear the details of any adultery.

Even if an adult child is already in the midst of a dispute, it's never too late to pull them out of it. It can be easy to slip into bitterness and recrimination. You can't be on your guard all the time. Remarks spoken to friends can be overheard. Comments that start out as an objective explanation of where you all find yourselves now can turn into something different when you are questioned or pushed by an anxious child. Start the process of putting it right by telling them you are sorry this has happened and that you will work hard to avoid it happening again.

Nobody's perfect so don't beat yourself up if these challenging goals don't always fall into place easily. The older the child, the more likely it is that they will be capable of looking to the future with optimism.

Action points

■ Set aside some time when you can speak to your children, however busy they are.

■ Encourage them to talk to friends.

■ Keep up their activities.

'My parents were in their early 60s when they divorced. It's a myth that their children cope better. My mum wanted me to be there for her, to help pick up the pieces... but she didn't give me much room to work out what on earth I felt about all of this. Actually, I was devastated and should have had more space to come to terms with it all.'
Alison, 40.

Summing Up

- Just because your children are older, it doesn't mean separation won't rock their world.

- Don't pull them into arguments with your former partner.

- Don't burden them with a new role or expectations that they can replace your partner in practical or financial matters.

Chapter Eight

The Role of Teachers and Other Professionals

A teacher's role

How can teachers support children?

The familiarity and security of a school environment can play a vital role in helping children come to terms with the divorce or separation of their parents. These days, schools are keen to promote how they work in partnership with parents and never is this more important than in times of family upheaval.

Teachers who continue to engage and stimulate children's achievements at school, as they would usually, are already going some way towards making children feel more at ease and that life goes on. As children adhere to their normal timetable of activities, their sense of routine is strengthened. This routine becomes even more important when, at home, it feels like the world is caving in and things seem so unpredictable.

It's also important that children whose parents have separated aren't made to feel different to their classmates. Teachers should be encouraged to avoid terms and labels for the family situation that can cause upset.

For example, these days it's not wise to refer to a child as coming from a 'broken home'. Nor is it safe to assume that everyone in the family has the same surname. School staff shouldn't ring home and automatically ask for a 'Mrs Higgins' when the mum in question either wasn't married to Mr Higgins in the first place or they have split up. These sorts of references may seem trivial and to some they will be, but to others they will cause offence, and they deserve as much respect as the next family.

Beyond continuing the everyday normality of school life, teachers can also:

- Pay particular attention to ensure the child continues to achieve to the best of their ability.

- Talk as much as they can – underlining positive messages that the children are getting at home, such as the separation really isn't their fault.

- Give them time and offer understanding – don't assume a child who acts out of character by attention seeking in the midst of a parental separation is simply being naughty.

- Step in to lessen the isolation – if a child is very sad at school, begins to shy away from involvement in activities and spends more time by themselves, then the teacher can help.

- Give the child a task or role, which maintains contact with their peers and other staff, such as collecting work when it's completed. Or the teacher could initiate certain work or projects to help the pupil continue to mix.

Secondary school teacher, Janet Murray, adds: 'It's really important that teachers stress to parents how important it is to keep in touch and keep the school up to date with contact details and addresses, as sensitively as possible.

'Sometimes parents get upset about letters not reaching them, but often it's because they haven't informed the school about addresses. It can all get a bit embarrassing for the staff who have to contact parents, especially if there's a problem and you have only got up to date contacts details for one parent – it can cause havoc!

'Also teachers need to be aware that children may have complicated living arrangements, for example co-parenting, where they spend half a week with each.

'Some kids try it on, saying they've left their books with their dad, or something. I always tell them that while I can appreciate it's more difficult for them to stay organised it isn't an excuse to forget their books or homework.

'I talk to them about how they can be more organised within the constraints of their situation, and help with reminders. But the bottom line is they have to be more organised than other kids and that's just the way it is.'

How can teachers support parents?

- Be understanding of the difficult times the parents are facing.
- Continue to welcome both parents into school to discuss their children's progress.
- Work together to tackle issues that arise.
- Provide information about how parents can continue to help their children in school.
- Encourage all parents to take an interest in their children's achievements.
- Talk as much as possible – to both parents.
- Provide equal access to reports, school records and parents' evenings.
- Ask the children whether extra copies of letters are needed – don't assume both parents will get to see the same one.
- Continue to involve a non-residential parent in any school activities such as sports day, craft competitions or field trips.
- Encourage all parents to continue activities to support schoolwork at home.

As a teacher, you should use your experience and knowledge of other families' situations to answer questions about the effect of separation on a child's development or academic progress, and encourage networking among parents.

Finding or strengthening a supportive group of friends or people who have shared the same life experiences can have a major positive effect on a parent's frame of mind after a separation. Schools can also offer ample opportunities for parents to meet and interact.

In class

Teachers should be encouraged to make their lessons as inclusive of children from all types of families as possible. As well as helping children from a family where the parents have been divorced, this can also promote understanding from their fellow pupils.

- Help children communicate.
- Boost confidence.
- Support positive parent-child relationships.
- Encourage understanding.

A solicitor's role

Do you think you need a solicitor? You may not.

But even if you have come to an agreement with your partner about what happens now and it all seems perfectly amicable, you may still want to get a second opinion.

A solicitor can tell you if what you have decided is fair and guide you on how to follow it through, ensuring that things remain amicable as circumstances change.

If you are still in the midst of agreeing about contact then a family lawyer can offer informed advice on what a court would make of it all, as well as guiding you through the process.

If you feel you need a solicitor then you can access those signed up to Resolution, an organisation committed to constructive and 'non confrontational' approachs to family disputes. Visit www.resolution.org.uk.

Resolution's code of practice includes putting the best interests of the children first and keeping financial issues separate. You can also find a wealth of information online about family law and some very useful frequently asked questions.

'My teacher
was an escape
to get to
school. I'm not
particularly
academic but
I loved being
somewhere
where every
moment wasn't
taken up
stressing over
what my mum
would be doing
next or what
dad's latest
misdemeanour
was supposed
to be.'

Thomas, 17.

Importantly, the 5,000 family lawyers who are members of Resolution are dedicated to keeping families out of court wherever possible.

'Mediation has much to recommend it – but where there is a history of domestic violence or abuse, or where one person refuses to co-operate, mediation will probably not be appropriate,' says Resolution Chair, Jane McCulloch.

'Members of Resolution all commit to discussing with their clients options like mediation and other ways of avoiding court. In fact over 90% of cases involving solicitors who are members of Resolution settle without going to court.

'Families come in all shapes and sizes and what is good for one isn't necessarily appropriate for another. What is important is that families are given the options and guided towards the process best suited to their individual circumstances,' Jane adds.

According to Resolution, a lawyer can help you sort out key issues including matters surrounding moving out of home.

So how can you find a solicitor that's right for you?

Always check that the solicitor you have in mind is a member of Resolution and has the bona fide professional qualifications and accreditations which allow them to practise in this highly sensitive area. (Stranger things have happened!)

You can have a short, initial session to see how you get on. Do not continue if you don't feel comfortable. Like any service provider, much of the relationship is based on whether you actually get on, so if a nagging voice tells you it's not right, get out.

What will a solicitor want to know?

Just as with so much else in the process of a divorce or separation, you have to plan ahead to make sure you get the most out of the situation. According to your unique circumstances and the urgency of the situation, your chosen solicitor will tell you what you should come to the meeting with. Take any extra paperwork relating to financial matters that you believe could be useful. Don't worry, it's better to go in over prepared than with too little information.

Remember in these circumstances, there is no such thing as a stupid question. Be clear in your mind what you want to ask and make sure you understand the answers. Take a note of questions you want to ask so that you don't forget them if you get nervous, and a pen and paper to record the answers so you can reflect on them before deciding on your next course of action.

The sadness and anxiety felt by parents or children in the midst and aftermath of a separation can lead to you seeking advice from your GP.

If you are clinically depressed then a range of options will be on offer, from cognitive therapy to anti-depressants – which in most cases will be seen as a last resort. You shouldn't feel that you are letting anyone down by going to see your doctor at this difficult time and you shouldn't beat yourself up for getting ill or 'not coping'.

'I was terrified of seeing a solicitor, I thought they would fleece me. Actually they suggested counselling.'

Sian, mum to Bryony, five.

Even the most capable of individuals can be plunged into despair when a marriage or relationship ends. Fearing that their children are also suffering is a huge burden to carry. In fact, those who have been successfully treated for depression are often keen to stress how the treatment worked for them – there is nothing to be ashamed of.

Just like adults, children can be prone to depression if they can't cope with those emotions. Healthcare professionals who work in the community or in schools may be trained to detect symptoms of depression in children and to assess those they feel may be at risk.

You may also want to enquire about counselling for your children, which will allow them to talk about how the divorce is affecting them and how they feel. Sessions can also include other members of the family or can be one-on-one. Counsellors will have a proposed session structure that can be tailored to individual family circumstances.

The emotions stirred up when children are attempting to come to terms with their parents' separation may mean that they have more contact with their GP. If you fear your child is depressed, then don't worry that taking them to the doctor will result in a diagnosis or prescription of anti-depressants.

Guidelines set down by the National Institute for Health and Clinical Excellence recommend what family doctors should and shouldn't do when treating children and young people with depression.

These guidelines say:

- Therapy should be offered as a first-line treatment.
- Anti-depressants shouldn't be offered to children with mild depression.
- Anti-depressants shouldn't be offered to children with moderate or severe depression except in combination with therapy.

Visit www.nice.org.uk for more information.

Depression affects around 1% of all children and 3% of adolescents. This includes reactive depression caused by a life-changing event such as the divorce or separation of their parents.

If left unchecked, depression in children can have a major impact on their ability to make friends, how they do at school and their self confidence. For all these reasons, if you genuinely believe your child may be showing signs of depression, you should take them to see your doctor. There is nothing to be afraid of.

At the very least, the doctor can talk to you about ways to help.

Family counsellors

Relate for Families has a number of services that are relevant for people experiencing a divorce or separation and want to get the best outcome for themselves and their children.

Relate is a service that makes children the centre of the process. The counsellor will help you protect your children from negative emotions, build strong plans for the future and seek the best solutions for contact with the other parent.

These sessions can help resolve practical and emotional issues. Relate's services aren't free but it is a not-for-profit service.

In general, counsellors can see those people affected by a separation either on their own, as part of a group or as a whole family.

The trained relationship experts encourage those taking part to voice their differences together – getting them out in the open. Having someone present who is an outsider or objective observer can be a real help and families find that they do open up in ways that they haven't experienced so far.

- The whole family.
- The parents.
- Brothers and sisters.
- Step-families.

More information is available through Relate's website at www.relate.org.uk.

What about a life coach?

You may have heard about the services of life coaches and some will specialise in relationships. This is a fast growing profession, where no qualifications are needed, so first things first – be cautious. If you are going to pay for a life coach – and many may charge on a daily or hourly basis – you have to be sure that they are the right one for you. You should not confuse the role of a coach with that of a therapist.

The coaches will ask questions and help you find the answers yourself. They can help you unlock the potential inside to find greater confidence and happiness, allowing you to relate more assuredly with your children, adapting to your new situation as best you can.

It's easy to be cynical, to seek to dismiss coaches as some symbol of 'new age' thinking that encourages self-indulgence. However, when you hear the success stories of such coaches and the people they have helped, it's hard not to be swayed.

Do your homework, find out about coaches in your area. Check out their testimonials and see how you get on. Quite often they may offer a session for free – what have you got to lose?

So how can a relationship coach actually help you? In her book, *Raising Happy Children for Dummies*, former deputy head Sue Atkins, who is now a coach, trainer and NLP practitioner, explains her approach.

She encourages parents to see things from their child's perspective. Sue says: 'I ask parents to place a piece of paper on the floor, step onto it, and imagine they're looking at the situation from the eyes of their child. I then ask them to answer the following questions as if they were the child:

What do you see and hear around you at the moment?

How do you feel?

How could mum and dad make you feel better?

What could they do or say?'

Reassurances and guarantees

Sue continues: 'I ask parents to write seven reassurances and guarantees that they can honestly give to their child. The reassurances and guarantees are things that will help their child cope with the enormous changes that are coming.

'Be honest – don't hedge around the difficulties. Don't give false promises that you can't keep because you destroy their confidence and belief in you at a critical time in your relationship. Give them information but not too much – give details of things in the not-too-distant future.'

Working together

Sue also helps parents develop some co-parenting strategies.

She says: 'Divorce changes – but it does not end – a family. Your children are now members of two families.

'A bad marriage can make parenting – and life in general – stressful. The loss of the family structure can be very upsetting and distressing for everyone involved in the major change.

'Despite divorce being on the increase around the world, parents often feel at a loss when searching for practical support. They also feel overwhelmed, confused, afraid, resentful, or completely frozen in panic about how to handle the changes in their family's way of life.

'Sometimes this fear manifests itself as animosity, which turns the whole divorce process into a battle, with children trapped in the middle and feeling

'Divorce needn't be like this. Parents can make positive, healthy choices during this very emotional time and make the transition less painful for everyone.

'Divorce isn't about winners and losers. It's about working out a way to handle the separation with dignity and compassion and minimising the disruption to your children emotionally. I offer numerous approaches and strategies for making the experience of divorce as positive and healthy as possible.'

You can read more about Sue on her website at www.positive-parents.com.

Action points

- Plan what you are going to say to your children's teacher.
- Continue to support your children with their homework and other out of school activities as much as possible.
- Check out counselling services in your area through Relate.

'I never dreamed I seeing a life coach, but they helped me remember the woman I am underneath, they gave me a new lease of life. I know some people will find this corny, but it worked for me. I know my children appreciate it.'

Annabella, mum to Harvey and Bradley, aged 11.

Summing Up

Teachers can offer support through a variety of means for children and parents. If you are a teacher, you should ensure that parents understand that even if they are no longer living with their children, it doesn't mean contact ends with their school.

Children can be encouraged to take part in activities to lessen any isolation they feel. If you fear that you or your child is depressed then you should seek medical help. Medication is a last resort.

Help List

Advice Now

www.advicenow.org.uk
Helps make sense of the law and your rights. Provides information on divorce and relationships.

BBC - Relationships

www.bbc.co.uk/relationships/couples
Provides tips to help with relationship issues, separation, divorce and step-families.

ChildLine

Freepost NATN1111, London, E1 6BR
Tel: 0800 1111 (24 hour helpline)
www.childline.org.uk
The free helpline is for children and young people in the UK. Call to talk about any problems with a counsellor.

Children and Family Court Advisory and Support Service (CAFCASS)

8th Floor, South Quay Plaza 3, 189 Marsh Wall, London, E14 9SH
Tel: 020 7510 7000
www.cafcass.gov.uk
CAFCASS looks after the interests of children involved in family proceedings.

Citizens Advice Bureau

www.nacab.org.uk.
Helps people resolve their legal, money and other problems by providing free information and advice from over 3,000 locations. Your local branch will be listed in the phone directory or you can search it using the search facility on the CAB webpage.

Directgov

www.direct.gov.uk
Provides legal information on separation and divorce.

Divorce Aid

www.divorceaid.co.uk

advice. Their volunteers provide support, advice and information.

Families Need Fathers (FNF)

134 Curtain Road, London, EC2A 3AR
Helpline: 08707 607 496 (6 pm – 10 pm week days)
fnf@fnf.org.uk
www.fnf.org.uk
FNF is a charity providing information and support on shared parenting issues arising from family breakdown. Their primary concern is the maintenance of the child's relationship with both parents.

Gingerbread

Tel: 0800 018 5026
www.gingerbread.org.uk
The largest membership organisation providing help for 1.8 million lone parents and their children throughout England and Wales.

Inside Divorce

Polyview Media, Hereford House, 23/24 Smithfield Street, London, EC1A 9LF
Tel: 020 7332 2572
www.insidedivorce.com
Information and support provided on a wide range of issues, such as relationship breakdown, moving on, divorce and separation.

National Domestic Violence Helpline

(run in partnership by Women's Aid and Refuge)
Tel: 0808 2000 247 (24 Help Line)
www.nationaldomesticviolencehelpline.org.uk
A national service for women experiencing domestic violence.

National Family Mediation

National Office:
Margaret Jackson Centre, 4 Barnfield Hill, Exeter, Devon, EX1 1SR
Tel: 01392 271610
www.nfm.org.uk
In Scotland:
Family Mediation Scotland, 18 York Place, Edinburgh, EH1 3EP
Tel: 0845 119 2020
www.familymediationscotland.org.uk
A network of local services which offers help to couples, married or unmarried, who are in the process of separation or divorce. Visit the national website for local offices in England and Wales.

National Mediation Helpline

Tel: 0845 60 30 809
www.nationalmediationhelpline.com
A service that explains the basic principles of mediation, answers general enquiries relating to mediation and puts you in contact with an accredited mediation provider.

The National Youth Agency

Tel: 0116 242 7350
www.youthinformation.com
Provides free information resources for young people. Areas covered include family, relationships, divorce and separation.

On Divorce

mail@ondivorce.co.uk
www.ondivorce.co.uk
This website provides lots of useful information on divorce, financial and legal matters. Includes case studies and an 'e-friends' page to allow people to share their experiences.

520 Highgate Studios, 53-79 Highgate Road, Kentish Town, London, NW5 1TL
Tel: 0808 800 2222
www.parentlineplus.org.uk
This is a national charity that works for, and with, parents.

Relate

Tel: 0300 100 1234
www.relate.org.uk
The UK's largest provider of relationship counselling. It offers advice, workshops, mediation, consultations and support.

Resolution

Central Office, PO Box 302 , Orpington, Kent, BR6 8QX
Tel: 01689 820272
info@resolution.org.uk
www.resolution.org.uk
Formerly known as The Solicitors Family Law Association, this is a large group of solicitors striving to resolve disputes in a non-confrontational manner.

Reunite

PO Box 7124, Leicester, LE1 7XX
Tel: 0116 2556 234 (advice line)
www.reunite.org
The is a leading UK charity specialising in international parental child abduction. It provides advice, information and support to parents, family members and guardians.

UK College of Family Mediators

Alexander House, Telephone Avenue, Bristol, BS1 4BS
Tel: 0117 904 7223
www.ukcfm.co.uk
This organisation provides information about family mediation, how to contact a family mediator and training for mediators.

Further Reading

Raising Happy Children for Dummies, Sue Atkins

What in the World Do You Do When Your Parents Divorce? A Survival Guide for Kids, Kent Winchester and Roberta Beyer

Since Dad Left, Caroline Binch

Shared Parenting, Raising your children cooperatively after separation, Jill Burrett and Michael Green

Divorce and Splitting Up (Which Essential Guides), Imogen Clout

Two of Everything, Babette Cole

Loving Yourself, Loving Another, Julia Cole

Two Homes, Claire Masurel and Kady Macdonald Denton

Truth About Children and Divorce: Dealing with the Emotions So You and Your Children Can Thrive, Robert E. Emery

When My Parents Forgot to Be Friends (Let's Talk About It!), Jennifer Moore-Malinos, Marta Fabrega

I Don't Want to Talk About It: A Story of Divorce for Young Children, Jeanie Franz Ransom and Katherine Kunz Finney

My Parents Are Divorced Too: A Book for Kids by Kids, Melanie, Annie and Steven Ford, as told by Jan Blackstone-Ford

Help Your Children Cope with Your Divorce, Paula Hall

Moving On, Suzie Hayman

Step Families, Suzie Hayman

Divorced Dad's Survival Book: How to stay connected with your kids, David Knox and Kermit Leggett

Was It the Chocolate Pudding? A Story for Little Kids About Divorce, Sandra Levins and Bryan Langdo

It's Not Your Fault, Koko Bear: A Read-Together Book for Parents and Young Children During Divorce, Vicki Lansky and Jane Prince

Starting Again, Sarah Litvinoff

Helping Children Cope with Divorce, Edward Teyber

Staying Together, Susan Quilliam

Putting Children First: A Handbook for Separated Parents, Karen and Nick Woodall

Need2Know

Need - 2 - Know

Available Titles

Drugs A Parent's Guide

Dyslexia and Other Learning Difficulties
A Parent's Guide ISBN 1-86144-042-1 £8.99

Bullying A Parent's Guide
ISBN 1-86144-044-8 £8.99

Working Mothers The Essential Guide
ISBN 978-1-86144-048-8 £8.99

Teenage Pregnancy The Essential Guide
ISBN 978-1-86144-046-4 £8.99

How to Pass Exams A Parent's Guide
ISBN 978-1-86144-047-1 £8.99

Child Obesity A Parent's Guide
ISBN 978-1-86144-049-5 £8.99

Sexually Transmitted Infections
The Essential Guide ISBN 978-1-86144-051-8 £8.99

Alcoholism The Family Guide
ISBN 978-1-86144-050-1 £8.99

Divorce and Separation Essential Guide
ISBN 978-1-86144-053-2 £8.99

Applying to University The Essential Guide

ADHD The Essential Guide
ISBN 978-1-86144-060-0 £8.99

Student Cookbook - Healthy Eating The Essential Guide
ISBN 978-1-86144-061-7 £8.99

Stress The Essential Guide
ISBN 978-1-86144-054-9 £8.99

Single Parents The Essential Guide
ISBN 978-1-86144-055-6 £8.99

Adoption and Fostering A Parent's Guide
ISBN 978-1-86144-056-3 £8.99

Special Education Needs A Parent's Guide
ISBN 978-1-86144-057-0 £8.99

The Pill An Essential Guide
ISBN 978-1-86144-058-7 £8.99

Diabetes The Essential Guide
ISBN 978-1-86144-059-4 £8.99

To order our titles, please give us a call on **01733 898103**,
email **sales@n2kbooks.com**, or visit **www.n2kbooks.com**

Need - 2 - Know, Remus House, Coltsfoot Drive, Peterborough, PE2 9JX